Original title:
The Plum's Promise

Copyright © 2025 Creative Arts Management OÜ
All rights reserved.

Author: Rory Fitzgerald
ISBN HARDBACK: 978-1-80586-289-5
ISBN PAPERBACK: 978-1-80586-761-6

Nature's Foretold Delight

In blossoms bright, a secret blooms,
The fruit has dreams, or so it assumes.
With every bud, a giggle sparks,
A dance of joy, in sunny parks.

The bees conspire in buzzing glee,
Whispering tales of what will be.
They tickle petals, who just can't wait,
For sticky fingers and juicy fate.

Echoing Gardens of Hope

In gardens lush, a chorus swells,
Tales of harvest that nature tells.
The soil chuckles beneath the sun,
As seedlings plot their playful run.

With every rain, a joke takes flight,
Dancing raindrops bring sheer delight.
Tiny fruits wear coats so bright,
Promising laughter, a tasty bite.

Euphoria in Sweetness

A fruit parade in summer's glow,
Each one boasts its cherry show.
With tiny hats and jaunty flair,
They beckon smiles from everywhere.

As shadows stretch and daylight fades,
The orchard hums in joyful shades.
A sweet revolt, small treats unite,
For giggles shared in crazy bites.

The Canvas of Orchard Dreams

In orchards wide, a canvas sprawls,
Where every fruit giggles and calls.
They share their plots of juicy schemes,
In colors bold like wildest dreams.

With painter's brush, a breeze will sweep,
The trees conspire, their secrets keep.
A splash of fun in every hue,
Promises sweet, and laughter too.

Circles of Growth

In the garden, mud pies sprout,
Little shoots laugh and shout.
Buds tickle the sun with glee,
Hoping one day to be a tree.

Worms wiggle in their squiggly dance,
While ants in a line take a chance.
Nature's circus, what a sight!
Frogs in top hats, jumping right!

Blossoms of the Future

In the springtime's wobbly breeze,
Flowers strut like they're at ease.
A daisy winks, an iris grins,
"Just wait for summer, let's begin!"

Bumbles buzz with tales so tall,
"Did you hear? We'll have a ball!"
Pollen parties, join the fun,
Under the rays of the golden sun.

Petals' Silent Vow

Petals giggle, soft and bright,
Hiding secrets from the night.
"Tomorrow we'll burst out in cheer!
Just wait for sunlight to appear!"

Buds whisper pink, yellow, and blue,
"A splash of color, look at us too!"
They promise to dance with the breeze,
As bees lend a hand, with such ease.

Juicy Whispers from the Vine

Grapes gossip under leafy shade,
"Next summer, look at the fun we've made!"
With plump laughter, they swell and grin,
"Soon we'll wear our fruity skin!"

The vine twirls, a winding maze,
"Join the harvest and let's amaze!"
Fruits will jive on picnic plates,
Sipping nectar, oh, how it slates!

Awaiting the Sun's Caress

In the shade, we play and joke,
With a fruit so round, we poke.
Silly hats and laughter ring,
Wonder what tomorrow will bring?

Clouds giggle as they drift and sway,
Whisper secrets of a bold sun's play.
We wait for warmth, don't be a bore,
My fruity friend wishes for more!

Time's Garden

In this garden, time spins fate,
Ticking slow, can't we just wait?
Watch the blooms dance, take a cue,
Fragrance sweet, oh what a view!

Rabbits hop, they tap their toes,
As sunflowers gossip, oh how it grows.
Would they share with us their cheer?
Bring more blooms to hold so dear.

Verses in the Orchard's Breath

Under trees where shadows sway,
We craft our rhymes in playful way.
With fruit as props, we take our stand,
Laughing while we make our plans.

Orchard whispers in breezy tones,
Telling tales in silly groans.
Who knew fruit could be so bright?
A circus show under moonlight!

Invitations from the Sky

Berries blush while clouds go by,
Inviting rain with a winked eye.
We dance below on grassy floors,
Hoping for drops, maybe more!

The sun hops high, its rays a tease,
Squirrels spin, oh, won't you please?
Catch the fun, let's make a toast,
For juiciness is what we'll boast!

Silent Transformations of Taste

In springtime's light, they dance and sway,
Little blossoms dreaming of their day.
Jokes abound in bees' buzzing flight,
Whispers of sweetness in sunlight bright.

With each playful breeze, they tickle the trees,
Delighting the sun with airy tease.
Ripening dreams, a trickster's delight,
Plump little orbs tease our appetite.

They hide in the shade, all dressed in their best,
In nature's own game, they never rest.
From tart to sweet, what a crafty jest,
A fruit in disguise, a true dining test!

So here's to the fruit with a smile so sly,
Nature's confetti, oh my, oh my!
With laughter, we gather and bite with glee,
Silent transformations, so glad, so free!

From Blossom to Essence

Once just a bud, now quite the tease,
A glimpse of the future on gentle breeze.
Pollen-tipped laughs, they giggle and grin,
As blossoms turn bold, it's time to begin.

The sun gets the joke, and the rain plays along,
In this fruity tale, nothing feels wrong.
With squirrels in the shade, all planning a feast,
Nature's own comedy, to say the least.

The blossoms transform, oh, what a sight,
From white to a blush, that's pure delight.
Juicy mischief hides in the green,
A reclusive act, fit for a queen.

So raise your glass to the playful shift,
From bud to the bite, what a wondrous gift!
In laughter, we savor this fruity fun,
A marvelous journey, oh, we've just begun!

A Palette of Flavor

In a bowl of colors, bright and bold,
The fruits are laughing, stories told.
Plums in purple, a mischievous grin,
Telling secrets on the wind's whim.

A splash of syrup, oh what a mess,
Sticky fingers bring such happiness.
Fruit salad dance, twirl and sway,
With each juicy bite, we giggle and play.

The Alchemy of Seasons

In spring's gentle breath, a riddle grows,
What hides in leaves? No one knows!
Summer's warmth turns whispers to shouts,
Blooming fruits know what it's about.

Autumn comes with a cheeky grin,
Harvesting laughter before winter's din.
With pies and jams, we toast the fun,
Savoring sweetness, one by one.

The Journey to Juiciness

A tiny seed with dreams so vast,
Wiggles through soil, growing fast.
Chasing sunshine, dodging rain,
Becoming plump—what a gain!

It rolls and tumbles, oh what a sight,
Ripening slowly, it's pure delight.
All on a mission to woo the taste,
Making jaws drop with every paste.

Seeds of Tomorrow's Feast

Digging in dirt, planting seeds with glee,
Hoping for wonders, oh can't you see?
Each little sprout, a comic delight,
Promising laughter from morning to night.

Future feasts in the garden wait,
Pickles and pies, oh isn't that great?
With every bloom, a party we'll host,
Celebrating joy, that's what we boast.

Prologue of Juiciness

In the orchard, shadows play,
A tease of sweetness, bright and gay.
The fruits are plotting, what a race,
To make us grin with juicy face!

Bouncing breezes, laughter loud,
Whispers of flavor, fun and proud.
With every drip, the giggles spread,
A syrupy joy, enough said!

When Blossoms Turn

Flowers giggle, in soft sunlight,
They promise fun, a sweet delight.
Pollinators dance, all in tune,
Making mischief under the moon.

Petals flutter, giggling bright,
Changing colors, such a sight!
Watch them morph with a little breeze,
Nature's jest, just to tease!

Echoes of Vitality

In every bite, a chuckle found,
Bursting laughter, joy unbound.
Fruitful echoes, a zesty cheer,
Punny flavors, come gather near!

With every squirt, the jokes unfold,
Silly stories, a taste of gold.
Zingy zest in a fruity jest,
Reviving spirits, that's the best!

Lush Dreams Await

In a garden, laughter weaves,
Fragrant fantasies bloom like leaves.
A juicy dream, ripe to explore,
Sweetened wishes, who could ask for more?

With each step, giggles unlace,
Splashing colors, a merry chase.
In every corner, fun's tucked away,
Harvest joy in a playful sway!

Beyond the Fertile Earth

In a garden far away, seeds had a scheme,
Hatching plans for a fruity dream.
With giggles and wiggles, they sprouted with glee,
But roots tangled up like they were at a spree.

The carrots told tales, the radishes roared,
While onions cried laughter, they couldn't ignore.
In rows they would dance, oh what a sight,
A veggie parade that lasted all night.

Leafy Dreams

Leafy greens hatched in their cozy beds,
Daydreaming big of fancy spreads.
With dreams of dressings and some fried cheese,
They plotted a feast that would surely please.

Lettuce in curls and salsa in swings,
Danced with tomatoes, oh, the joy it brings!
The greens twirled and spun, what a grand show,
With cabbage as DJ, they stole the whole glow.

Sunlight's Embrace

Sunshine peeked in with a sparkle and cheer,
Plants giggled softly, "The warmth is right here!"
They stretched out their leaves, basked in delight,
   Singing their songs in the morning light.

"Photosynthesis party, don't get too close!
We're glowing and growing — isn't that gross?"
Yet flowers were blooming, all bright and bold,
   With pollen that tickled, like stories retold.

The Dance of Seasons

Winter brought ice, a frosty affair,
The plants bundled snug, as if in a bear.
But springtime arrived with a giggle and wiggle,
Plants jumped for joy, oh how they did jiggle!

Summer got sassy, with sunburned leaves,
"Forget the sunscreen!" they laughed in the breeze.
But fall had the last laugh, with colors so bright,
"Let's paint the world, what a magical sight!"

Savoring Sun-Kissed Delights

Under the sun, they dangle bright,
A juicy joke, they roll in sight.
With each ripe bite, a laugh does swell,
In every crunch, a tasty spell.

Sweetness drips on summer's cheek,
A fruity giggle, oh so sleek.
All gather round to share the glee,
In orchard's realm, we dance with glee.

Cradled by Boughs

Beneath the branches, laughter grows,
Swirling with breezes, we strike a pose.
The fruit is prime, a silly prize,
Making faces, we munch and rise.

With every toss, we aim and cheer,
A sticky challenge, never clear.
Oh, how they bounce, these merry fruits,
In playful chaos, we chase our boots.

Tales of the Orchard's Heart

Gathered round, with tales to share,
The funny fruits, they dance with flair.
A jester's hat, a juicy disguise,
In every bite, the orchard cries.

Whispers of sweetness, a chuckle blooms,
With every crunch, humor looms.
Outrageous flavors, bold and bright,
Spill the secrets of delight.

The Flavor of Hope

In laughter's hue, the fruits do gleam,
A whimsical orchard, a silly dream.
Odd shapes and colors, so grand to see,
With each sweet taste, we feel so free.

Hope bubbles up like fizzy cheer,
A fruity wish in every sphere.
Beneath the leaves, our giggles soar,
In this grand garden, we crave for more.

Secrets of the Orchard

In a tree, there hangs a fruit,
With giggles sounding, oh so cute.
The bumblebees all dance and sway,
While squirrels plot to snatch away.

The leaves whisper tales of taste,
A secret stash no time to waste.
With every bite, a chuckle bursts,
As juice dribbles—oh, how it thirsts!

The sun peeks through with playful glee,
While shadows dance like wild esprit.
Each fruit a smile, each branch a jest,
Eating them—well, it's quite the quest!

So join the fun and take a bite,
Let laughter fill the orchard bright.
For in this place where mischief's grown,
The sweetest joys are always shown.

Blossoms of Hope

In springtime's jest the buds unfold,
Dressed in colors bright and bold.
A bee gets stuck in petals tight,
The flowers laugh at his plight!

Dancing in fields, the blossoms cheer,
As clumsy critters wander near.
A rabbit hops with such great flair,
But trips and lands—oh, poor—beware!

The breeze comes in with ticklish charms,
Rustling leaves with whispering arms.
Each bloom a promise, giggles shared,
In joyful chaos, none are scared.

So wander here where laughter grows,
In petalled pockets, love still flows.
For every bloom that twirls so free,
Brings silly smiles to you and me.

The Harvesting Heart

With baskets brimming, off we go,
To find the fruit that's ripe and low.
A friendly raccoon steals a treat,
And scampers fast on tiny feet!

The laughter echoes through the glade,
As silly games of tag are played.
A scarecrow winks with button eyes,
While pumpkins grin at all the highs.

In every row, adventure calls,
With tangy bites that thrill and brawl.
We stumble upon a hidden stash,
And squeal with joy as we make a splash!

So gather round, and don't be shy,
With every harvest, let laughter fly.
For in these fields, where fun is king,
Each heart retrieves a joyful fling.

Nectar's Vow

As bees convene with buzzing flair,
They take their vows with spicy air.
Each droplet glistens, sweet, divine,
While ants form lines to mark the sign!

A flower mumbles, "What a sight!"
As butterflies flaunt wings of light.
With nectar trails, their festival,
Leaves no doubt—it's a carnival!

And as the sun starts to dip low,
The critters gather, putting on a show.
A ladybug breaks out in dance,
While fireflies twinkle, lost in trance.

So sip the sweetness from the bloom,
As laughter wafts like a fragrant plume.
In every drop, a giggle found,
Nectar's joy is all around!

Branches of Aspiration

In a tree that sways with glee,
A fruit dreams of being free.
It hopes to dance on summer's breeze,
And giggles with the buzzing bees.

With each sprout, it plots a scheme,
To roll down hills and chase a dream.
A juicy batch of sun-kissed fun,
Sipping nectar till it's done.

But oh! The squirrel looks so sleek,
With acorn plans, it starts to speak.
'Hey there, buddy, don't you fret,
Your time will come, you can bet!'

So the branches sway and laugh along,
As each one hums a silly song.
In the orchard's merry cheer,
Tomorrow's harvest is held dear!

Ripened Dreams

A round red dream hung high and proud,
Amongst the leaves, it feels so loud.
It whispers tales of pies and jams,
While plotting escape from fruit-loving clams.

With visions of sassy, sweet delight,
It practices its 'look at me' flight.
'Catch me if you can, my friend!'
Giggles ring out as the fun never ends.

A slice of life, it hopes to be,
In breakfast bowls, where it can see.
With berries, cream, what a party scene,
Who knew being fruit could be so keen?

But wait! What's that? A cookie's glance,
Rallying troops for a bold romance.
'Let's unite and bake with flair,
A dessert that loves to share!'

Sunkissed Expectations

Under the sun, expectations bloom,
Eager to break free from their gloom.
They giggle and nod, with heads held high,
Imagining parties, oh my, oh my!

'We'll be bright in a bowl or jam,
Turned into treats, oh yes, ma'am!'
So they stretch and soak, catching rays,
Dreaming of sweet and merry days.

But wait! Here comes a pie crust, round,
Promising sweet glory all around.
'Oh cherries think they own the stage,
This is our moment, turn the page!'

With laughter high in fruity cheer,
Expectations burst, let's make it clear!
For every slice, a giggly grin,
In the garden of sun, let's dive in!

Garden of Tomorrow

In the garden where dreams take flight,
Fireflies dance in the soft twilight.
Each sprout tells jokes of what's to come,
A future full of laughter and fun!

'What if I turn into a pie?'
A cabbage chuckles, 'Oh me, oh my!'
While carrots wager on a stir-fry,
The lettuce laughs, 'Well, I can fly!'

'Let's make a salad that will stun!
With croutons here, and dress it up fun!'
Equality reigns in this veggie chat,
With all flavors wrapped in a hat.

Tomorrow's banquet, oh what a tease,
Where each grows giddy in the breeze.
With bowls of joy and plates that sway,
The garden giggles, 'Let's save the day!'

A Tribute to the Immature

In a bowl they sit, so round,
Not a care, they giggle and bound.
"Why wait to swing, or climb a tree?"
With juice on their face, they frolic with glee.

The world is big, yet they stand small,
They roll away, never heed the call.
"Maturity? Not our style!"
They laugh and play in their own sweet mile.

For too soon they'll face the grind,
But today they shake off the bind.
"Let's dance in circles, let's not grow!"
The vision of adulthood, a perplexing show.

So here's to those in their prime,
Making messes, feeling sublime.
Life's not bitter, it's ripe and sweet,
In every folly, they find their beat.

Borne on a Breeze

A breeze blew by, a funny sight,
Plums dancing high, in pure delight.
They twirled and laughed in the summer sun,
"Catch us if you can! Oh, this is fun!"

They floated past, those plump little spheres,
Singing a tune that tickled our ears.
"We're not just fruit; we're a comedy!"
With each jaunty bounce, they held a spree.

In the orchard, chaos gave a cheer,
Daring the wind to come hover near.
"Step right up for a fruity ride!"
With a giggle, the plums took pride.

So if you spot them, don't just stare,
Join the dance, feel the warm air.
For in their play, there's joy to seize,
Life's full of laughs, just like the breeze!

Manifesting Joy

In a world of green, they sit and scheme,
Plucky young plums make a silly dream.
"We'll be ripe, and then we'll shine!"
With cheeky grins, they sip on sunshine.

They play in the trees, throw leaves in the air,
"Who cares about ripeness? We just don't care!"
With every wobble, they claim their fate,
"We'll manifest joy while we're still on the plate!"

The sun does shine, but they won't rush,
Pretending to be in a hasty hush.
"No time to fret, we're on this ride,"
With giggles galore, they won't be inside.

So wave your arms, let them all see,
Joy's in the journey, wild and free!
In every swirl, a chuckle takes form,
Among the branches, we'll bend and swarm.

Harvesting the Future

Gather round, the fruit parade,
Juicy tales in the sun they've made.
"We're the future, ripe and bold!"
With laughter loud, their stories unfold.

A harvest dance, bright and silly,
Each plump plum says, "Aren't we frilly?"
"Watch us bounce, don't miss the show!"
With every giggle, their ambitions grow.

Planning futures with pom-pom cheers,
Daring the world to lend an ear.
"We'll teach the seeds how to tease the light,"
With mischievous grins, they take on flight.

So let them tumble, let them sway,
In each mistake, there's a brand new way.
For harvesting joy is a fine affair,
When laughter's the crop, and love's in the air!

The Fertile Promise

In the garden, a joke is sprouting,
A fruit so silly, no doubt about it.
It dances in the breeze, a sight to see,
Whispering secrets to the buzzing bee.

The blossoms giggle, their petals shy,
Hiding from the sun, oh my, oh my!
They wear tiny hats, just for fun,
Waiting for the day they get to run.

With every raindrop, they bounce with glee,
Plotting grand adventures, oh so cheeky!
Their roots are tickled, their leaves all swirl,
Dreaming of becoming a fruity girl.

So raise a glass to this silly thing,
A toast to fruits that laugh and sing!
May they roll the dice and take their chances,
In the garden where joy forever dances.

Horizon of Riches

In a field of dreams, the sun does beam,
A crazy fruit with a wobbly gleam.
It wears a crown of leaves so fine,
Claiming it's richer than wine!

With every breeze, it shakes and jives,
While all the birds roll their little eyes.
"Look at that fruit, trying to impress!"
Squeezed into laughs, it's such a mess.

The clouds all chuckle, the earth shakes free,
As this fruit bounces with utmost glee.
Riches of laughter in every bite,
At the horizon of silly delight.

So gather around for a fruit parade,
Where every chuckle and grin is made!
With our funny fruit, let's share the cheer,
In this horizon, laughter's clear!

Fruits of Anticipation

Oh, the fruits that wait with such delight,
Their dreams are marinated, oh what a sight!
Wrapped in whispers of every breeze,
Chasing laughter, climbing trees.

They stretch and yawn, as time drags on,
Telling stories from dusk till dawn.
With every tick, they wiggle and twist,
Plotting how to become the sweetest bliss.

Anticipation's the name of the game,
Every fruit wishes to earn its fame.
They plan a party, inviting all,
For the day they drop, and have a ball!

So laugh along with the fruits that wait,
As they dream big on this wild fate.
With every giggle, they break the mold,
In this fruity story, let joy unfold!

Nectar of Tomorrow

Adventures await in the nectar so sweet,
A fruit with a secret, ready to greet.
It teases the sun with its cheeky glow,
Waving hello to the world below.

With drops of laughter, it fills the air,
Telling tales of joy without a care.
It dreams of being a smoothie true,
With a sprinkle of fun, just to woo you.

When morning breaks, and the dew is fresh,
This fruity delight declares it's enmesh.
With bubbles of giggles and secrets to share,
The nectar flows freely, filling the air.

So sip the sweetness and dance in the sun,
With the nectar of tomorrow, joy's never done.
Boosting laughter with every drip,
In a world where fun takes a funny trip!

Fruitful Whispers

In the garden where fruits giggle,
The pears told jokes, the apples wiggle.
Bananas slipped on laughter's bark,
While berries danced till it was dark.

Citrus tossed zesty puns around,
Even lemons couldn't frown—not a sound.
Cherries winked, sparkling with delight,
Swaying in tandem, feeling just right.

A shy grape sprouted a tiny grin,
Barely bursting with laughter within.
Each round fruit shared their secrets so sweet,
In whispered giggles, they couldn't be beat.

So raise a cup of juicy cheer,
To the fruits who bring laughter near!
For life's too short to take a seat,
Let's dance like fruits, with laughter replete!

Beneath the Lush Canopy

Under the shade where giggles grow,
Fruits plot mischief in a row.
Grapefruits tease with sour wit,
While oranges bounce in a citrus fit.

Kiwi hides, thinking it's sly,
As pears conspire, oh my, oh my!
Banana jokes split the afternoon,
Chuckles blending with the tune.

Ripe berries hold a silly play,
Drama unfolds in a fruity way.
Peaches ponder plots so grand,
As cherries join with a fruity band.

And when the sun dips low to rest,
They sing their tales and feel so blessed.
So here's to laughter under trees,
Where nature's humor sways in the breeze!

A Sweet Destiny

In a world where sweetness reigns,
Fictional fruits trade funny gains.
A melon claims it runs a shop,
While prunes insist, "We never stop!"

With every joke they pulse and roll,
As strawberries pare their heart and soul.
The puns flow thick like syrupy cream,
Truth and laughter, a wild dream.

Ripe figs float with a gentle hum,
While pineapples bring the beat of a drum.
Grapes confide their secret schemes,
Mixing catchphrases and sweet drinks' dreams.

And in this fruity carnival bright,
Every bite reveals laughter's light.
For life's a feast, let's celebrate,
In this orchard where giggles await!

Beneath the Ripened Skin

Underneath skins so vibrant and bright,
Fruits reflect chuckles under the light.
An apple quipped, "I'm the fairest, you know!"
While nuts snickered at their own show.

A peach made faces, trying to tease,
As berries burst out, "Let's not freeze!"
Tangerines tumbled in rounds of fun,
Playing games till the day was done.

Grapes worked hard to win the prize,
With punchlines tucked in clever replies.
Even lemons couldn't hold their cheer,
As laughter ripened in every sphere.

So lift your hearts and raise the cheer,
To the fruits that make humor clear!
Their juicy tales forever be spun,
In this funny world where we all run!

Nature's Sweet Oath

In the orchard, blossoms tease,
Fruitful jokes dance on the breeze.
Leaves whisper secrets, pink and bright,
Nature grins in morning light.

Bumblebees buzz a silly tune,
Chasing rays from the afternoon.
Tree limbs sway with playful cheer,
A fruit-filled future, loud and clear.

Silly squirrels leap and play,
Waiting for their fruity payday.
Underneath the skies of blue,
Nature laughs; it knows what's due.

So here's to the fun that comes our way,
With blossoms bright for another day.
Nature's secret, sweet and sly,
Harvest dreams beneath the sky.

Hues of Anticipation

Under sun, the colors blend,
Ripeness waits 'round every bend.
Cherry reds and brilliant hues,
All await their day to cruise.

Grasshoppers hop with comic flair,
Jumping snacks without a care.
Birds sing songs of fruity fate,
Imagining a grand old plate.

In their laughter, voices ring,
Nature's promise makes them sing.
Yellow light falls on the green,
Painting plump dreams in between.

The trees chuckle, rustle leaves,
Time for fun before it weaves.
With every breeze, the whispers call,
For nature's feast, the grandest ball!

Sweetness in the Breeze

A breeze of sweetness fills the air,
As fruits get ready for a dare.
Each one winks, a little tease,
Promising a taste that will please.

Fluffy clouds drift, share a grin,
While cheeky robin does a spin.
Nature's party starts to swell,
As blossoms bloom, there's fun to tell.

Bears and deer peek in delight,
Wondering when the snacks take flight.
Berry bowls in wild design,
Waiting for the season's wine.

So gather near, the fruit is ripe,
With nature's lore, it's time to swipe.
With giggles shared, we toast the trees,
To sweetness wafting in the breeze!

Glistening Potential

In sunlight's hug, bright gems appear,
Fruitful dreams are drawing near.
Buds are bursting, laughter's stored,
Promising a playful hoard.

Jellybeans in leafy green,
The sweetest sights you've ever seen.
Critters gather, all in line,
Eager for their taste divine.

Around the world, a plucky dance,
From tree to tree, a bouncy prance.
Every rustle, every sway,
Sprinkles fun in nature's play.

Heed the whispers in the glen,
All await the fruit again.
In each shimmer, nature grins,
For sweetness, life joyfully spins!

The Lure of Juicy Wisdom

Beneath a tree so grand and wide,
A squirrel plots with juicy pride.
"Why pick a grape?" he quips with glee,
"When plump delights await in me!"

A wise old owl, perched high in thought,
Chimes in with lessons life has taught.
"Don't rush to taste what's near your hand,
Sometimes, the best things need a stand!"

The sun above, it beams and glows,
While tiny ants in chorus croak.
"Don't judge a fruit by its bright hue,
A little patience brings the dew!"

So heed the tales of orchard lore,
Where laughter echoes, wisdom roars.
And if you seek a tasty bite,
Remember, not all gems are bright!

Shadows of a Fruitful Future

In gardens where the shadows play,
A funky gnome will dance all day.
"What's ripe and round will surely fall,
But watch your head, it's a juicy ball!"

Beneath the leaves, where secrets lie,
A critter snickers, oh my, oh my!
"Dream big, my friends, with all your heart,
You'll harvest laughs before you start!"

Bees buzz about with tiny tunes,
While sunflowers swaying hum like loons.
"Plant your dreams, let them take flight,
In shadows, fruit glows oh-so-bright!"

So sip the nectar, sweet and cool,
Join in the fun, you silly fool!
For every joke that you will share,
Will lead to treasures born from care!

Tales from the Orchard

Once in an orchard, plump and round,
There lived a pear who wished to pound.
He danced and jived with a jolly crew,
  Proclaiming, "Juice is what we brew!"

The apples laughed, with eager cheer,
"Join the fun, there's nothing to fear!"
While berries burst in colorful streaks,
Whispering dreams through cheeky peaks.

The bushes huddled, sharing about,
The wild escapades when fruits go out.
"One splash of juice can change the day,
  So dip and dive in berry fray!"

Each tale spun bright beneath the sun,
Where laughter reigned and all were fun.
In every fruit, a story awaits,
  From garden beds to orchard gates!

The Weight of Abundance

When branches bow with juicy weight,
A giggling lemon seals its fate.
"I'm zesty, yes, and looking fine,
But all this gold? It's all divine!"

Around the trunk a grape parade,
With plump intentions, grandly laid.
"Roll with it, friends, don't be forlorn,
Life's a feast from dusk 'til morn!"

A pumpkin plods, with glee he sways,
"My size is great, in many ways!
But oh, the weight can make me tire,
I dream of being a sweet squire!"

In harvest's grace, the laughter spills,
As apples dance on rolling hills.
And though the load may seem a chore,
Together we thrive, forevermore!

Capturing Sunshine in Flesh

Underneath the leafy dome,
A little fruit wants to roam.
It's giggling with a plump delight,
Ready to spark joy at first bite.

With cheeks so round and skin so bright,
It's a dance in the golden light.
Each squishy hug, a fruity cheer,
Whispers of joy, like summer here.

In orchards where the critters play,
They plot the sweetest heist each day.
A game of tag with bees in flight,
Fruits laughing through the warm twilight.

So squeeze me tight, dear sun-kissed friend,
This fruity fun will never end.
From tree to mouth, a tale so grand,
Together we shall joyfully stand.

Unwritten Chapters of Fruity Bliss

Oh juicy tales of life untold,
In every bite, a story unfolds.
Sweet whispers shared on picnic blankets,
With cheeky giggles and sticky spankets.

The fruit parade begins to march,
With a spread of laughter, oh what a starch!
Pies and jams, oh what a scene,
We're making memories, sweet and obscene.

Bouncing berries in a bowl of fun,
Chasing their friends beneath the sun.
An adventure in every juicy drop,
Where belly laughs just never stop.

So let's write tales of fruity cheer,
With every slice, the joy is clear.
The chapters grow with every taste,
In this fruity world, there's never waste.

Echoes of Earth's Bounty

In the garden where giggles grow,
Fruits waltz as breezes blow.
With their blushing cheeks on display,
They plot a sweet escapade today.

They whisper secrets to the bees,
While dodging leaves on the playful breeze.
Bounding 'round the vibrant vines,
They're counting hugs and fruity fines.

Each pit a laugh, each skin a grin,
With every bite, the fun begins.
They cheer for summer, toast for fall,
With joyful echoes, we hear them call.

So dip your fingers in this sweet cheer,
For bounty lingers, never fear.
In every fruit, a joke is spun,
Echoes of laughter, second to none.

Layers of Flavorful Fate

In the kitchen where chaos reigns,
Fruits are plotting their tasty gains.
With layers stacked, they dance about,
Making it messy, without a doubt.

They twirl in bowls and giggle in pies,
With sneaky smiles and watchful eyes.
A sprinkle of sugar, a splash of zest,
Flavorful fates put to the test.

Mixing dreams with a dash of cheer,
As laughter bubbles, drawing near.
With every chop and joyful slice,
They know their sweet destiny is nice.

So let's blend them up without delay,
Into a treat that's here to stay.
For in this mix, a wealth of fun,
Flavorful fates—our victory won.

The Delicate Balance of Life

In the garden, fruit takes a stand,
Dancing on branches, so carefully planned.
A squirrel swoops down, quite bold and spry,
Stealing my treats, oh me, oh my!

The bees buzz around, in sweet delight,
Mixing up nectar, in morning light.
They hum a tune, a wacky song,
As I chase them around all day long!

The sun winks down, a golden ray,
Telling the fruits, it's time to play.
But watch out, dear seeds, don't get too sly,
Or you'll end up baked in Grandma's pie!

So here we are, the fruits and I,
Living this life, oh me, oh my!
Balancing sweet and tangy delights,
Making each day a fruity fight!

A Promise Beneath the Skin

Under the surface, secrets lie,
In every wrinkle, a cheeky spy.
With such promise, a fruit would glow,
But first, it has to learn to grow!

The rain drops down, a splashy dance,
Encouraging roots to take their chance.
But a hefty wind comes, laughs so loud,
Yanking my plump friends from their proud crowd!

With each twist and turn, fate does reign,
What once was sweet might find it plain.
Just one bad joke from a cheeky crow,
And off they tumble in a fruity show!

Yet hidden inside the skin so bright,
Lies a promise that feels just right.
When life gets nutty, and the skies turn gray,
Remember, my friend, enjoy the fray!

Alluring Horizons of Fruit

Bright colors beckon, oh what a sight,
Rolling in laughter, day turns to night.
Peaches and cherries in a juicy race,
Can you blame them for the smile on their face?

They whisper sweet secrets, oh so grand,
Of summertime fun and a picnic planned.
But then a raccoon takes a funny leap,
Patching the fruits while they rest in sleep!

Rolling and tumbling, they've lost their grace,
Chasing each other, what a wild chase!
Once they were firm, now they get so mushy,
Thanks to the critters who envision a slushy!

But look at this chaos, the laughter we find,
Sharing the fruit with a humorous grind.
So here on the horizon, so fruity and bright,
Each laugh, a promise, to savor the night!

Nature's Ritual of Ripeness

With a wink and a nod, nature does act,
Teaching the fruits with wisdom intact.
Every droplet counts in this silly play,
Turning green dreams into a juicy buffet!

The dance of the leaves keeps rhythm in time,
While critters conspire with a cheeky rhyme.
A rabbit hops in with just the right scheme,
To join the fruit party, it seems like a dream!

Every blush of color, a cue to pop,
With flavors that twirl, you just can't stop!
But don't get too comfy, oh little pear,
The cook is in waiting with fiery glare!

So ripen away, in the sun's warm hug,
Enjoy every moment, let life give a tug.
For when the season ends, don't cry or pout,
Laughter is sweeter, without a doubt!

Blossoming Potential

In a garden full of glee,
A tree bursts forth with jubilee.
Buds giggle in the sunny light,
A fruity joke, oh what a sight!

Squirrels whisper to the breeze,
"Is it time for jam or cheese?"
A dance of petals, sweet and spry,
They leap like clowns across the sky!

Branches swing, they're feeling bold,
With promises of treats untold.
A fruit parade is on its way,
Anticipate the playful play!

So watch them grow, those silly fruits,
With all their laughs and leafy suits.
For in this plot of merry cheer,
Each burst of color sings—time's near!

Thickets of Anticipation

In thickets dense, a secret bides,
Cheeky vines where laughter hides.
The fruits, they plot their grand debut,
In curly twists, they laugh anew.

A daffodil, with nose held high,
Shouts, "I'm ripe! Come taste, oh my!"
The bees just buzz, they can't believe,
What wild stunts the trees conceive!

The bushes jig, the leaves all sway,
Puns and giggles light the way.
"Just wait," they say, "we'll bring some cheer,
A juicy joy that's almost here!"

In every branch, a joke found new,
The humor's bright, the vibes are true.
So pluck a laugh from nature's play,
The fruits declare, "Let's rule the day!"

A Bounty of Possibilities

A basket sits, it's rather spry,
Filled with dreams that dance and fly.
Each glossy side a perfect tease,
A farmer's grin is sure to please!

Apples whisper, "Pick us first!"
While pears yell out, "Don't quench your thirst!"
"Are we all in this together?
A fruity team—oh, what fun weather!"

With every bounce, a fruit takes flight,
Will cherries tiptoe through the night?
The melons roll, a slippery sight,
As flavors mingle, pure delight.

So harvest laughs from orchard dreams,
With juicy schemes and funny themes.
Each plump delight, a game to win,
A quirky tale that makes us grin!

When Blossoms Call

When blossoms call, come one, come all,
To petals beckoning with a brawl!
They sway and laugh in colors bold,
With promises of fruits untold.

"Who'll taste the pie? We're ripe!" they tease,
While wind whispers through budding trees.
"Join in the fun, let's throw a riot,
A juicy joke—you'll love to try it!"

The laughter spreads through sunny air,
As budding fruits declare their flair.
"Let's have a feast, a fruity spree,
Forget your worries, just come see!"

So gather ye glad and merry folk,
Let's dance and caper, share a joke!
For as the blossoms bloom and sway,
They bring us joy, the fruity way!

Bonds of Sun and Soil

In a garden where laughter grows,
Sun's tickle sparks the roots below.
Wiggly worms dance with delight,
While daisies giggle in morning light.

The carrots wear shades, looking bold,
As radishes boast their stories untold.
With beetroot blushing, they all agree,
Life's a party, come plant with me!

Twirling vines in playful sprawl,
Chasing shadows, having a ball.
Earthworms slide, they're slick and fun,
Soil and sun, a race well-run!

As blossoms bloom in clumsy grace,
The garden sings, a joyful place.
With every sprout, a grin appears,
Nature's humor, through the years.

Slow Embrace of the Season

Seasons flirt like lovesick fools,
Chasing each other, breaking the rules.
Winter throws snowballs, spring's in a whirl,
While summer sun twirls in a graceful twirl.

Frog in the pond croaks silly rhymes,
While daisies nod with their bright, sunny chimes.
The breeze tells jokes, tickling the air,
As flowers bloom with a mischievous flair.

Leaves crack a smile as colors fly,
Yellow and orange like a pie in the sky.
As clouds tumble, twinkling with glee,
Nature's own comedy, wild and free.

Each season wraps in a warm reprise,
With fruits and laughter, the world's own prize.
And as the sun dips, don't pout or mope,
Tomorrow's a giggle, a garden of hope.

Reaching for the Sun

With arms outstretched, a leafy crew,
Standing tall, like they bid adieu.
Say goodbye to the gloomy gray,
And hello to the rays of the playful day.

Little sprouts stretch, feeling so grand,
Imagining their future, so well-planned.
Dreaming of heights where butterflies roam,
Their dance is a song, and the wind is home.

Sunflowers wink as they sway and twine,
While grasshoppers hop, claiming good time.
Each petal a smile, each leaf a cheer,
Life's a big joke, and nature's the dear.

Under the blue, they giggle and laugh,
The warmth is a spell, a vibrant gaffe.
So reach for that sun, and don't hold back,
Life's too short; let's have a laugh!

Yet to Ripen

Green and round, they play a game,
Holding secrets, without any shame.
"Oh, we're tasty!" they tease and taunt,
Just waiting for sunbeams, they do flaunt.

With every drip of morning dew,
They giggle softly, in shades of true.
"Come on, you sunshine! We know you're near,
We're peachy keen, just give a cheer!"

Ripe dreams dangle, just out of touch,
With every glance, they grow too much.
"I'm bigger than you!" the berries shout,
While figs giggle, "You have your doubts!"

Yet to ripen, they've secured their clout,
With laughter ringing, they laugh it out.
Under the sky, waiting with glee,
They know the best things come for free!

Rippling Through Time

In a garden where jokes bloom bright,
The fruit whispers tales of delight.
With each pluck, a giggle's found,
As laughter ripples from ground to ground.

The squirrels join in with acorn hats,
While birds crack wise with cheeky chats.
A wobbly dance in the sunny shine,
As the fruit flirts with the notion of wine.

Bumbling bees buzz with comic flair,
They trip on petals, unaware of air.
Each fruit a jester, ripe and round,
In this orchard, silliness is crowned.

So grab a slice of nature's jest,
Where every laugh gives nature rest.
With humor tucked in each juicy edge,
Come join the fun, no need to hedge.

Beyond the Green Horizon

Where green meets blue, tales grow tall,
With fruit-shaped dreams that dare to sprawl.
Each bite a burst of laughter's tease,
Tasting the sun as we bask in the breeze.

The grass wearing shades, a quirky sight,
As critters dance in pure delight.
Unlikely friendships bloom anew,
In the shade where giggles break through.

A sunbeam tickles a cheeky chad,
As fruit declares it's never sad.
Wobbling shapes on the vine they tease,
Making sure the world bends with ease.

Beyond horizons of emerald dreams,
Laughter flows like vibrant streams.
In this realm where jeers entwine,
Every fruit whispers, 'Life is divine!'

An Ode to Summer's Glow

Oh summer, you sizzle with playful flair,
Tickling toes and sun-kissed hair.
With fruits that burst and laughter spry,
Under the wide and laughing sky.

Picnics line the shaded spots,
With fruit in hats, yes, they're in knots!
Each chuckle tangles in the air,
As bees do a jig without a care.

The sun winks down as it splashes gold,
While fruit on branches tell tales bold.
They promise nectar, juicy and sweet,
As we dance to nature's off-beat beat.

Oh laughter, a summer's loud decree,
Fun and frolic, wild and free.
With every slice, a joy we sow,
In a whimsical world where giggles glow.

Nature's Patient Heirloom

Beneath the leaves, in whispers divine,
The treasures wait, as stars align.
With roots wrapped tight in mystery's song,
Nature grins, oh, it won't be long.

Each fruit a gem, with tales to spin,
Of weathered smiles and cheeky grins.
The earth rolls with laughter and glee,
As it shares its riches with you and me.

A slow parade of juicy mirth,
As critters revel in the soil's worth.
Old trees chuckle at time's own pace,
While seeds play hide and seek in the race.

So trust in the crops, let patience reign,
For laughter blooms in sun and in rain.
In nature's quilt, so earthy and bright,
An heirloom of humor, pure and light.

Dreaming of Sweet Harvests

In the garden where dreams align,
I spotted a fruit that whispered, 'I'm fine!'
With a wink and a twist on the vine,
I laughed at my luck—what a marvelous sign!

Beneath the sun with a mischievous grin,
Those fruits sang 'come on, take us for a spin!'
But their prickly laughter made me think twice,
Are they sweet little gems or just tempting spice?

When they tumbled down with a plop and a bump,
I danced around hoping none would go thump.
Yet one little guy rolled right to my feet,
Said, "Pick me up, I'm the life of the treat!"

So I gathered my treasures, all shiny and bright,
Promised to savor with all of my might.
In this fruit-laden dream, oh what a delight,
I chuckle, "Who knew fruit could spark such a flight?"

Beneath the Tender Skin

Peeling back layers, a giggle erupts,
What's hiding inside? Just a bunch of plups!
They tumble and jostle, a fruity parade,
Whispering secrets in zesty charades.

Beneath that soft skin, a story unfolds,
Of sweetness and laughter, as each tale is told.
I pondered their journeys, the fun they had,
And wondered if they ever felt sad.

I reached for a bowl, so shiny and round,
To catch all their giggles, the laughter they'd found.
Yet as I dug in, they squealed a dismay,
"Hey, watch it now! We're not for display!"

So we formed a new pact, a merry old crew,
To jiggle and bounce, just for the few.
With each tender bite, sugar treasures I'd find,
Beneath the soft skin, oh, what a fun kind!

Whispers of Ripening

Oh, the tales that the branches do tell,
Of fruits in the sun, sweetening well.
They whisper of flavors, some silly, some bold,
And share how they dream of being sold!

Just the other day, one boasted a flair,
"I'm the sweetest around, take a whiff if you dare!"
While another chimed in with a chuckle and sigh,
"Sure, but I'm juicy enough to make grown men cry!"

And what's this about skins, soft as a tease?
They squawked and they squabbled, "Oh please, oh please!"
With every ripe moment, laughter was near,
They twirled in the breeze, spreading joy and cheer.

So gather around, for the harvest is bright,
With whispers of ripening, pure delight.
In this playful orchard, laughter does reign,
A fruity fiesta, forever untamed!

Secrets in the Orchard

In the secret of groves, where the fruits like to play,
They scheme and they giggle, hey, what do they say?
"I'm round, I'm fine, and I promise a zinger,"
"Just wait till you taste me, oh boy, I'm a singer!"

Underneath playful leaves, they share funny lies,
Of mischievous ants and runaway pies.
"I'll bounce off your spoon," one fruit did declare,
While another rolled down, and I felt the air flare.

In this orchard of wonders, a festival blooms,
Where flavor and laughter lift up all the fumes.
Let's concoct a wild pudding, a giggly delight,
With cherries and laughter—the future seems bright!

And as we indulge, with sprinkles and all,
The secret of fruit is to always have a ball.
For in each silly bite lies a treasure of fun,
In the heart of this orchard, we're all number one!

Veins of Enchantment

In the orchard, secrets bloom,
Squirrels plan, they plot their room,
Fruit so sweet, they can't resist,
Nature's snack? A juicy twist.

Feathers flit, a cheeky crew,
Chasing tales, as daylight grew,
Ripe delights hang from their thrones,
While bees buzz contradicting tones.

Who knew berries wore such flair?
Wobbling round without a care,
Laughter echoes with each fall,
The grandest feast, come one, come all!

In this garden, mirth takes root,
With every prance, a windblown fruit,
So come and join the merry feast,
Where joy and oddity are released.

Shadowed by Sunlight

Shadows dance upon the grass,
As fruit glows bright, they sneak and pass,
Jokes are shared, a sunny jest,
Under the branches, all are blessed.

Lemonade laughs, lemonade spills,
While silly squirrels hunt for thrills,
Chasing tales in the summer air,
Spotting juicy treasures bare.

Under leaves, the shadows play,
Mocking sunbeams, come what may,
Tickling tendrils, sweet and sly,
While tiny birds take a side-eye.

Oh, the games this landscape weaves,
As nature giggles, and often deceives,
Sunshine plots the playful schemes,
And fruit-filled laughter fills our dreams.

A Dance of Petals and Pits

Petals flutter, a twirling spree,
With each leap, they sing with glee,
Dropping laughter in the breeze,
A fruity waltz among the trees.

Gathered close, each pit did cheer,
As blossoms hoot with facetious leer,
Dancing round in grand parades,
Nature's jesters all displayed.

Tiny bumbles join the fun,
Bopping along, they weigh a ton,
Hilarity bursts in fragrant air,
A fruity fest, who wouldn't dare?

So let the petals guide your feet,
In this zany, joyful beat,
For every spin, a chuckle bright,
As nature dons her colorful light.

Farewell to Winter's Grip

Winter bids a frosty cheer,
As fruit springs forth, the warmth is near,
Funny hats on leafy heads,
Mirth encircles like flowing threads.

Gone are snowballs, now we've fruit,
With ice cream dreams, it'll be a hoot,
The sun laughs loud, melting woes,
While flavor dances, up it goes!

Chasing warmth, the seedlings call,
Each sprout a jester at the ball,
With every bud, a joke takes flight,
As winter bows to spring's delight.

So say goodbye to frosty feet,
Join the pie-baking, joyous beat,
For laughter thrives where blossoms burst,
In this garden, humor's first!

Where Colors Merge

In a garden where colors collide,
A jellybean tree grew too wide.
Its branches danced in the summer breeze,
Playing hide and seek with the bumblebee.

A parrot squawked jokes up high,
While the carrots plotted how to fly.
A rainbow slipped on a slip of ice,
And tumbled into a bowl of rice.

Sunflowers wore glasses, quite the sight,
Painting rainbows from morning light.
Each laugh echoed, a cheerful map,
Where colors merge and giggles clap.

Lemons started a comedy show,
As cucumbers danced in a row.
In this wacky garden so bright,
Every shade swirled, a delight!

Beneath a Lush Canopy

Beneath the leafy, leafy dome,
The squirrels staged their wild home.
They crafted swings from vines and cheer,
While ticklish breezes wandered near.

A rabbit in shades sipped tea with pride,
As a dancing potato rolled aside.
The sunbeams giggled, tickling the ground,
In laughter's echo, joy was found.

The apples wore hats, oh what a sight,
And cherries debated the best dance bite.
With every rustle, tales took flight,
Beneath the canopy, pure delight.

The mushrooms held parties after rain,
While toadstools grinned without a grain.
Their secret dances made the moon sway,
In the leafy home where pranks play!

Sunkissed Promises

In a town where fruit dreams collide,
Ripe oranges painted the landscape wide.
The sun played tricks, a playful tease,
Turning lemons into pockets of ease.

Bananas slipped on puddles neat,
While grapefruit twirled on wobbly feet.
The peaches grinned, their laughter bright,
Filling the air with pure delight.

Grapes wore capes, oh what a show,
Swinging from vines, high and low.
With each gleam of the sun's warm grace,
Sunkissed promises filled the space.

Cherries played cards under the tree,
Laughing at jokes, as happy as can be.
In this fruity land, with smiles galore,
Sunkissed secrets opened the door!

Morning Dew on Fragile Dreams

At dawn, when the world wore its gown,
The flowers whispered, never a frown.
With morning dew, they danced and spun,
Spreading giggles under the sun.

A caterpillar in pajamas sat,
Complaining about the late-night chat.
The lilacs chuckled, sweet and bright,
As dandelions took off in flight.

Bumblebees buzzed, a comical crew,
Trying to fit in a morning brew.
Mimicking birds, they sang with glee,
In a parade of absurdity.

With fragile dreams floating on air,
Each drop of dew held laughter rare.
Morning's embrace, so fresh and warm,
Nurtured joy, a sweet charm!

A Promise in Bloom

In a garden bright, where fruits take flight,
A little plum jokes, 'I'm almost right!'
She stretches and yawns, under the sun's glance,
Saying, 'Please give me space, I'm applying for pants!'

A squirrel stops by, with a wiggle and spin,
'Is that a fruit? Or just a cheeky grin?'
The plum giggles loud, 'Oh, I'm totally fine,
Just here waiting for summer, and maybe some wine!'

Fat bees buzz around, sharing sweet praise,
They dance and they twirl in the warm sunny rays.
'You'll be delightful,' they say with a cheer,
'But first, hit the gym, we recommend a few leaps this year!'

So here's to the fruit, with her snazzy facade,
Growing plump and absurd, it isn't that hard!
In the world of delights, she'll shine, oh so bright,
With a wink and a smile, a juicy delight!

Echoes of Sweetness

In the orchard's embrace, oh what a sight,
Juicy gems dangle, ready for bites.
Yet a chubby plum grins, 'Here's my big chance,
To turn into jam, and have a grand dance!'

With a giggle and jiggle, she sways on a branch,
'Thought I'd make cider, but I missed that chance!'
The scarecrow just chuckles, hoping for pie,
'I'll save you a spot, when you're sweet and spry!'

Bouncing around, in a bright summer sun,
The plums play a game; who's heavier? Fun!
Laughing so hard, as they tumble and drop,
'Find me a bucket, oh goodness, we plop!'

And as the day wanes, the stories unwind,
Of plummy adventures, and growing combined.
So if you see them, just know it's a play,
These fruits of delight, making giggles each day!

The Touch of Late Summer

As summer takes hold, the sun waves its wand,
Plums grow like balloons, each one of them grand.
A fluffy little bug remarks with delight,
'You look just adorable, let's take a flight!'

They hatch a big plan, to go on a spree,
Rolling down hills, oh what fun it'll be!
The plums shout in laughter, 'We're flying, oh no!
Just a squishy fruit, with a gravity show!'

The breeze starts to tease, 'Watch out for the birds!'
But plums just roll on, ignoring the words.
With courage and cheer, they bounce and collide,
'This fruity delight train has nowhere to hide!'

So next time you see, a fruit filled with zest,
Know laughter and joy are in every quest.
For summer's sweet touch brings giggles so bright,
And fruits with a promise of laughter and light!

Unraveled Secrets

In the orchard hush, secrets float on air,
'What's that?' says a plum, with a wobbly stare.
A whispering breeze carries tales of the day,
Of plums planning mischief in a fruity ballet!

'Let's spill the beans, about the pie we could make!'
Said one cheeky fruit, who had a wild shake.
The others all giggle, 'Oh, what a mess!
Just think of the crumbs! It'll be such a stress!'

But still they conspired, to bake up a plot,
For a flaky delight that would sizzle a lot.
With laughter a-plenty, they cooked and they stirred,
These plums were once shy, now the quirkiest herd!

The oven erupted with giggles so bright,
A burst of sweet joy, a truly great sight.
So here's to the plums, with secrets now shared,
Creating a feast, and a fun that is bared!